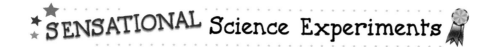

★SENSATIONAL Science Experiments

Far-Out Science Projects with Height and Depth

How High Is Up?
How Low Is Down?

Robert Gardner

Enslow Publishers, Inc.

40 Industrial Road   PO Box 38
Box 398   Aldershot
Berkeley Heights, NJ 07922   Hants GU12 6BP
USA   UK

http://www.enslow.com

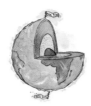

Library of Congress Cataloging-in-Publication Data

Gardner, Robert, 1929-
   Far-out science projects with height and depth : How high is up? How low is down? / Robert Gardner.
      p. cm.
   Includes bibliographical references and index.
   ISBN 0-7660-2016-9
   1. Mensuration—Experiments—Juvenile literature. 2. Altitudes—Measurement—Experiments—Juvenile literature. [1. Altitudes—Measurement—Experiments. 2. Measurement—Experiments. 3. Experiments. 4. Science projects.] I. Title.
   QA465 .G25   2003
   530.8'078-dc21
                                              2002004619

Printed in the United States of America

10 9 8 7 6 5 4 3 2 1

To Our Readers: We have done our best to make sure all Internet Addresses in this book were active and appropriate when we went to press. However, the author and the publisher have no control over and assume no liability for the material available on those Internet sites or on other Web sites they may link to. Any comments or suggestions can be sent by e-mail to comments@enslow.com or to the address on the back cover.

Illustration credits: Tom LaBaff

Photo credits: © Corel Corporation, pp. 26, 27, 28, 29 (background); National Oceanic and Atmospheric Administration (NOAA), pp. 26, 27, 28, 29.

Cover illustrations: Tom LaBaff

Contents

(Experiments with a 🎗 symbol feature **Ideas for Your Science Fair**.)

Introduction

Height and Depth All Around You

How high are the clouds or the tree in your yard? How deep is a pond or a page of this book? There are so many things to measure in the world around you. This book can get you started investigating height and depth. You will learn how to measure some common things around your home using a ruler, a meterstick, or a yardstick. Perhaps after doing some of the experiments you will want to do more and more measuring. You may come up with a great idea for a science fair.

Entering a Science Fair

Some of the experiments in this book might give you ideas for a science fair project. Those experiments are marked with a ⚜ symbol. Remember, judges at science fairs like experiments that are imaginative. It is hard to be creative unless you are interested in your project. So pick a subject that you enjoy and want to know more about.

You can add to the value of the experiments you

do by keeping notes. Set up an experiment notebook and record your work carefully. As you do some of these experiments, you will think of new questions that you can answer with experiments of your own. If you have ideas for new experiments, then try them (with your parents' or teacher's permission). You are developing the kind of curiosity that is shared by all scientists.

If you enter a science fair, you should read some of the books listed in the back of this book. They will give you helpful hints and lots of useful information about science fairs. You will learn how to prepare great reports that include charts and graphs. You will also learn how to set up and display your work, how to present your project, and how to talk with judges and visitors.

How to Measure

In this book you will be measuring heights and depths. To make these measurements you will use a ruler and a meterstick or yardstick.

Rulers may have either metric units (millimeters, centimeters, meters) or U.S. Customary units (inches, feet, yards), or both. The ruler in drawing **(a)** has metric units. The distance between the small, closely packed lines is one millimeter, or mm. The distance between the numbered, longer lines is one centimeter, or cm.

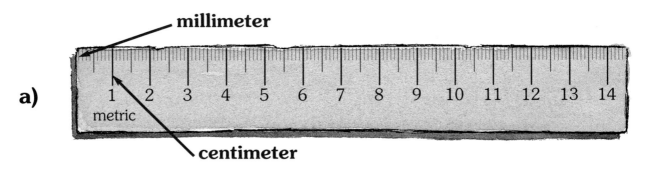

millimeter

a) metric

centimeter

As you can see by counting, there are 10 millimeters in *every* centimeter, so:

$$\textbf{1 centimeter = 10 millimeters}$$

Drawing **(b)** shows the ends of a meterstick, a wooden rod that is 1 meter long. As you can see, there are 100 centimeters in a meter. That can be written:

1 meter = 100 centimeters

b)

meterstick

There are 1,000 millimeters in 1 meter, so:

1 meter = 100 centimeters = 1,000 millimeters

Drawing **(c)** shows a 6-inch ruler. The distance between each numbered line is 1 inch. Each inch is divided by lines into halves (1/2), quarters (1/4), and eighths (1/8) of an inch. Some rulers, like this one, are even divided into sixteenths (1/16) of an inch.

c)

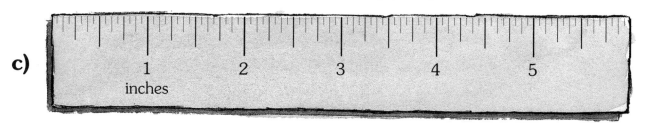

Two 6-inch rulers placed end to end would be one foot because:

12 inches = 1 foot

Drawing **(d)** shows the ends of a yardstick, a wooden rod that is 36 inches, or 1 yard, long. There are 12 inches in 1 foot, so a yard is 3 feet long.

d)

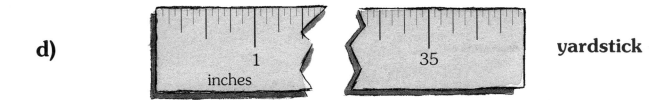

yardstick

1 yard = 3 feet = 36 inches

Drawing **(e)** shows how a metric ruler can be used to measure something. Because the end of a ruler is sometimes worn, it is best to start measuring at the clear line above the 1-centimeter mark. The object shown, as you see, is 4.5 centimeters long.

e)

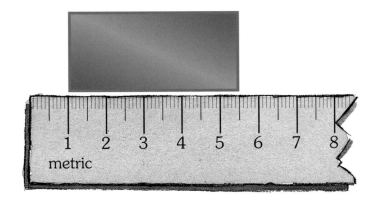

Safety First

As you do the activities and experiments in this or any other book, do them safely. Remember the rules listed below and follow them closely.

1. Any experiments that you do should be done under the supervision of a parent, teacher, or another adult.

2. Read all instructions carefully. If you have questions, check with an adult. Do not take chances.

3. If you work with a friend who enjoys science too, keep a serious attitude while experimenting. Fooling around can be dangerous to you and to others.

4. Keep the area where you are experimenting clean and organized. When you have finished, clean up and put away the materials you were using.

How Tall

Sometimes it is easy to find out how high or tall something is. Sometimes it is not so easy. You will start with something easy. How tall are you?

Let's Get Started!

1. Ask a friend to help you. Take off your shoes.

2. Tape a sheet of paper to a door frame. The center of the paper should be about as high as the top of your head.

3. Stand very straight with your head up and your back against the door frame. Have your friend hold a ruler or yardstick across the top of your head. The ruler should be level, with one end against the paper. The person holding the ruler on your head can mark with a pencil where the ruler touches the paper.

Things you will need:
- ✔ friend
- ✔ tape
- ✔ sheet of paper
- ✔ door frame
- ✔ ruler or yardstick
- ✔ pencil
- ✔ metersticks, yardsticks, or tape measure
- ✔ parents or friends

Are You?

The distance from the floor to the mark on the paper is a measurement of your height.

4 Using one or two metersticks, yardsticks, or a tape measure, find your height. How tall are you in centimeters? In inches? In meters and centimeters, in feet and inches?

How tall is the person who helped measure your height? How tall are your parents? How tall are your friends?

Idea for Your Science Fair
If you own a pet, how can you discover how tall your pet is? At what place on the animal do you measure its height?

How High Is

The ceiling in your home or school is higher than the top of your head. But how high is it? And how much higher than the top of your head is it?

Let's Get Started!

1. Hold one meterstick (or yardstick) against a wall so that its end touches the ceiling. If you need a stepladder because the ceiling is very high, **ask an adult to help you**.

2. Place the end of a second meterstick against the bottom of the first one. (You may have to do this again if the ceiling is more than 3 meters high.)

3. Use the first meterstick (or yardstick) to measure the distance from the floor to the bottom of the second stick. What is the height of the ceiling in centimeters? In inches? In meters and centimeters, in feet and inches? How much taller than you is the ceiling?

Ideas for Your Science Fair

If you live in a house or apartment with several floors, do the ceilings on all floors have the same height?

Your Ceiling?

How do the ceiling heights in different buildings compare? What is the most common height for ceilings?

If there is a basketball hoop at your school, can you find how high above the court it is?

How High Are

How high is a flight of stairs in your home or school? Can you measure the height of the stairs the same way you measured your height?

There is a practical way to measure the height of stairs. Stairs are made of steps and risers. The steps are separated by risers as shown in the drawing. All the risers have the same height. You can find the height of the stairs by making one measurement, counting, and multiplying.

Let's Get Started!

1. Measure the height from one step to the next. If the front of the step is round, put a ruler flat against the higher step. Use another ruler to measure the distance from the lower step to the higher one as shown.

2. Count the number of risers.

3. Multiply the height of one step by the number of risers.

Height of flight of stairs = (height of one step) x (number of risers)

Why will this multiplication give you the height of the flight of stairs?

Your Stairs?

Ideas for Your Science Fair

Can this method be used to find the height of a spiral stairway?

The Washington Monument in Washington, D.C. is approximately 169 meters (554 feet) tall. You can walk to the top using its 898 steps. Assume the monument rises 10 meters (33 feet) above the last step. Using a calculator, figure out the height between each step. (See answer on page 45.) How does that height compare with the height between the steps in the stairs you measured?

step

riser

How High Is

A roof's peak is higher than a ceiling within it. How high is it to the peak of your house or school?

Let's Get Started!

1 Count the number of rows of shingles, clapboards, bricks, concrete blocks, or other materials on the outside wall. Usually these rows all have the same height. Count the number of rows from the bottom layer to the peak of the roof.

2 Measure the height of a single row.

3 Multiply the height of one row by the total number of rows. What is the height of the outside wall cover?

Your Roof?

④ Part of the foundation may be seen below the outside wall. If so, measure the height of the foundation from the ground. Add the height of the foundation to the height of the outside wall. How high is the peak of your house or school?

Things you will need:
✔ school building or house
✔ pencil and paper
✔ ruler

The siding of my house is made of shingles. There are 50 rows of shingles to the peak of my roof. A 6-inch-high board can be seen above the shingles and just below the roof's peak. Each row of shingles is 5 inches high. One foot (12 inches) of the foundation can be seen above the ground. The peak of my roof, therefore, is:

Height of roof = (height of shingles x number of rows) + height of board + height of foundation

(5 inches x 50) + 6 inches + 12 inches = 268 inches, or 22 feet 4 inches.

How high is the peak of your roof? (You may have to measure the inside height of your attic to find the peak of your roof. **Ask an adult to help you.**)

How High Is

One way to find a flagpole's height involves measuring shadows—those of some stakes and the flagpole's.

An object twice as tall as another will cast a shadow twice as long. An object three times as tall will cast a shadow three times as long and so on.

Let's Get Started!

1. Take two stakes, one about twice as tall as the other. Using a hammer or mallet, drive them into the ground beside each other on a sunny day. Measure their heights. If one is not twice as tall as the other, drive one of them in some more.

2. Measure the shadows of each stick. You will see that the taller stake's shadow is twice the length of the shorter stake's shadow.

3. Now you will find the flagpole's height. Drive the longer stake into level ground next to the flagpole. Measure the length of the stake's shadow. Cut a strip of cardboard that length. Count the number of times

a flagpole?

the cardboard fits onto the flagpole's shadow, as shown in the drawing. The flagpole's shadow is this many times longer than the stake's shadow.

4 How tall is the stake? Measure the stake. Now you can find the height of the flagpole.

$$\text{Height of flagpole} = \left(\begin{array}{c} \textbf{number of times} \\ \textbf{cardboard fits on} \\ \textbf{flagpole shadow} \end{array} \right) \times \textbf{(height of stake)}$$

How tall is your flagpole?

Ideas for Your Science Fair

How could you use shadows to find the height of a tree?

Figure out another way to find the height of a flagpole. Is your method easier or more difficult than measuring shadows?

How High Is

You used shadows to find the height of a flagpole. You can use the same method to find the height of a tree. But there is another method you can use, even on a cloudy day.

Let's Get Started!

1 Have a friend stand next to a tree. Stand about 20 meters (60–70 feet) from your friend.

2 Hold a pencil upright at arm's length in front of one eye. Close the other eye. Place the top of the pencil in line with the top of your friend's head. Hold the pencil steady. Move your thumb along the pencil until it is in line with the bottom of your friend's feet. The distance between your thumb and the top of the pencil represents your friend's height as seen from where you are.

3 See how many times your friend's height fits into the tree's height. To do this, move the pencil upward along your view of the tree one length at a time.

4 Measure your friend's height. Then you can find the tree's height.

$$\text{Height of tree} = \left(\begin{array}{c}\textbf{number of times}\\ \textbf{friend fits in tree}\end{array}\right) \times \left(\textbf{height of friend}\right)$$

a Tall Tree?

Ideas for Your Science Fair

How tall is the tallest tree you can find?
On average, are certain types of trees
(maple, birch, or oak) taller than others?

Things you
will need:
- ✔ tree or tower
- ✔ pencil
- ✔ meterstick,
  yardstick, or
  measuring tape

How High Is

An aneroid barometer measures air pressure. It has a can from which the air has been removed. Changes in air pressure make the can expand or contract. Its change in size is magnified by levers connected to a pointer by a chain. The pointer moves over a dial that measures pressure. (The dial may indicate air pressure in centimeters or inches of mercury, or in millibars.)

The atmosphere is like an ocean of air. After you dive deep into water, you can feel the pressure decrease as you come to the surface. The same is true of the atmosphere. As you go up into the air, the pressure decreases because there is less air above you. Your ears may "pop" as they sense the change in pressure.

Let's Get Started!

1. To find the height of a mountain use your aneroid barometer to measure air pressure at the base of the mountain.

2. **With an adult**, take the barometer to the top of the mountain. How much less is the pressure at the top of the mountain?

Things you will need:
- ✔ aneroid barometer
- ✔ mountain
- ✔ an ADULT
- ✔ pencil and paper

3️⃣ Near Earth's surface, air pressure decreases about 1 inch of mercury for every 300 meters, or 1,000 feet of height. Use this information to estimate the height of the mountain you went up.

Height of mountain = $\left(\begin{array}{c}\text{decrease in air pressure} \\ \text{in inches of mercury}\end{array}\right)$ x 300 meters

You can estimate the height of clouds if you know what kind they are. Clouds are classified by the way they look.

Stratus clouds are wispy, foglike, and often produce a drizzle. They may begin as ground fog and rise 30 to 150 meters (100 to 500 feet). They often cover parts of tall buildings and hills.

Stratocumulus clouds are dark gray but seldom produce rain. They are often rounded or wavy and cover most of the sky. Usually, they are at heights of 450 to 2,000 meters (1,500 to 6,500 feet).

stratus clouds

Nimbostratus clouds are dark and produce continuous rain, sleet, or snow. They stretch upward from as low as 30 up to 900 meters (100 to 3,000 feet).

Cumulus clouds are fair-weather clouds that look like puffy, white cotton balls.

stratocumulus clouds

Low Clouds?

They are usually at heights of 600 to 3,000 meters (2,000 to 10,000 feet).

Things you will need:
✔ clouds

On warm, humid days, cumulus clouds may grow into **cumulonimbus** clouds, or thunderheads. These clouds are filled with rain or hail. Their lower dark parts stretch upward from about 1,500 meters (5,000 feet) to white, triangle-shaped tops that may reach heights of 15,000 meters (50,000 feet).

Let's Get Started!

1 Observe low clouds when they appear. Use the information here to estimate their heights.

nimbostratus clouds

cumulus clouds

cumulonimbus clouds

The height of high clouds can also be estimated from the way they look.

Altocumulus clouds are rounded, fleecy, grayish clouds. They occur at about 3,000 meters (10,000 feet).

Altostratus clouds have a dull, grayish-blue look. When seen through these clouds, the sun or moon looks like it is broken into tiny pieces. These clouds are found at heights of 4,500 to 6,000 meters (15,000 to 20,000 feet).

A sky covered by white, patchy **cirrocumulus** clouds is often called a "mackerel sky." The clouds are so called because from the ground they look like fish scales. Cirrocumulus clouds are usually at a height of 5,500 to 6,000 meters (18,000 to 20,000 feet).

Cirrostratus clouds look like nearly see-through white

altocumulus clouds

altostratus clouds

High Clouds?

veils. They often cover the sky and cause a halo to form around the sun or moon. These clouds are usually about 6,000 meters (20,000 feet) high.

Cirrus clouds look like white featherlike tufts or threads. They are made of tiny ice crystals. Cirrus clouds are often called "mares' tails" because they look like horses' tails. These clouds are usually found at heights of 6,000 to 12,000 meters (20,000 to 40,000 feet).

cirrocumulus clouds

Let's Get Started!

① Observe high clouds as weather patterns change. Find clouds like those shown here. Use the information to estimate the heights of the clouds.

cirrostratus clouds

cirrus clouds

How Do We Know

One way the heights of clouds are found is by flying airplanes through them. But how does a pilot know how high the airplane is?

The pilot could use an altimeter. An altimeter reads height from changes in air pressure. Another kind of altimeter uses radar to measure height. A pulse of radio waves is beamed toward the ground. The waves reflect from the ground and are picked up by instruments on the plane. The time for the pulse to travel from the airplane to the ground and back is measured. Knowing that time, the plane's height can be found.

Radio waves travel at a speed of 300,000 kilometers per second (186,000 miles per second). Therefore, it takes a very short time for the pulse to travel to the ground and back.

To see how this method works you can use sound waves.

Cloud Heights?

1 Find a big building with metal or brick siding. Stand about 50 meters (55 yards) from the building.

2 Clap two wooden blocks together to make a loud sound. Listen for the echo. The time between sound and echo is the time for the sound waves to go to the building and back. Sound travels at about 330 meters (1,100 feet) in one second. For sound to travel to the building and back, it should take less than half a second. Does that seem about right for the sounds you heard?

Things you will need:
✔ big building with brick or metal siding
✔ 2 wooden blocks

31

How Deep Is

① Using a ruler, find out how deep this book is from the top of the front cover to the bottom of the back cover. How deep is it?

② How deep are all the pages in this book? To find out, measure from the bottom of the top cover to the top of the bottom cover.

Things you will need:
✔ ruler
✔ pencil and paper

③ Here is a more difficult question. How deep is each of the book covers? To find out, you can subtract the depth of all the pages from the total depth of the book. Then divide that number by two. (There are two covers.)

Suppose the depth of the entire book was 31 millimeters and the depth of the pages was 25 millimeters. Then the depth of the covers would be:

31 millimeters – 25 millimeters = 6 millimeters

Then the depth of one cover would be:

6 millimeters ÷ 2 = 3 millimeters

What did you assume in finding the depth of one cover? (See answer on page 45.)

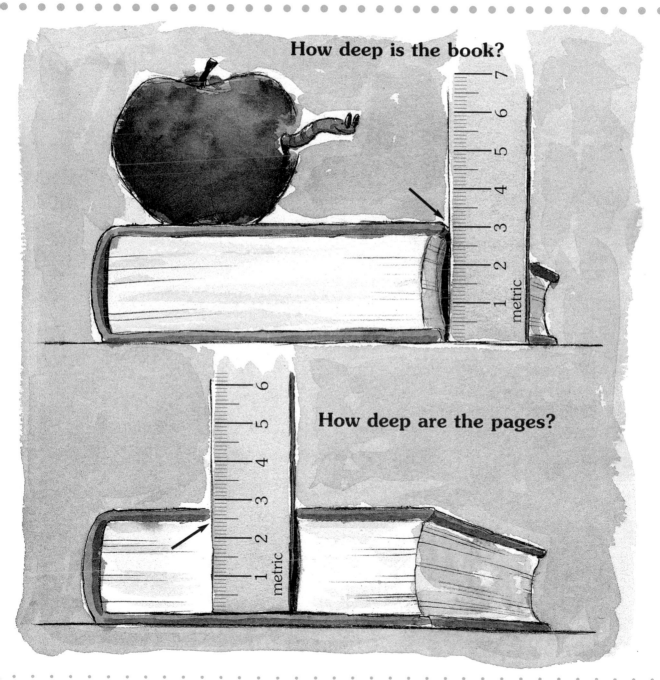

How deep is the book?

How deep are the pages?

How Deep Is

Y ou cannot measure the thickness of one sheet of paper with a ruler. Can you think of a way to measure the thickness of a single sheet?

Remember how you found the height of a stairway. You measured the height of one step. You then multiplied that height by the number of risers.

Let's Get Started!

1 To find the thickness of a sheet of paper, you can measure the thickness of many sheets; then divide by the number of sheets.

Suppose a book contains 250 pages. You measure the thickness of the 250 numbered pages and find it to be 15 millimeters. Print is found on both sides of the sheets, so 250 page numbers means there are 125 sheets, because: **250 ÷ 2 = 125.**

To find the thickness of one sheet, divide 15 millimeters by 125 sheets. If you do this on a calculator you will find that:

15 millimeters ÷ 125 sheets = 0.12 millimeters per sheet

Since 0.1 is equal to 1/10, the sheets are a little more than 1/10 of a millimeter in thickness.

One Page?

How deep is one page of this book?

Idea for Your Science Fair

Do the pages of all books have the same depth? How can you find out?

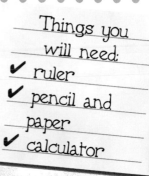

Things you will need:
- ✔ ruler
- ✔ pencil and paper
- ✔ calculator

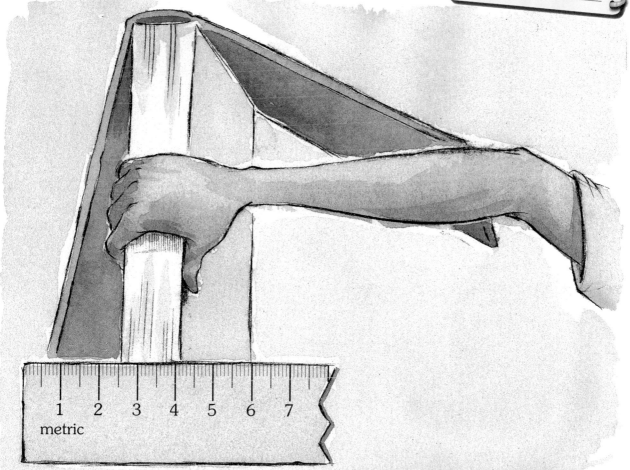

How Deep Is

1 Before you take your next bath, use a ruler to find the depth of the water in the tub. **Ask an adult** to supervise you. How deep is the water?

2 Is the water the same depth at both ends of the tub? If not, can you explain why the water is deeper at one end than at the other?

Your Bathtub?

Things you
will need:
- ✔ ruler
- ✔ water
- ✔ an ADULT
- ✔ bathtub

3 What happens to the depth of the water when you sit in the tub? Can you explain why the depth changes? How much does it change?

How Deep Is

The stairs leading to a basement are made of steps and risers. One way to find the depth of a basement is to measure the height of the stairs leading to the basement. You did that earlier in this book. You measured the height from one step to the next. You then counted the number of risers and multiplied the height of one step by the number of risers. But there is another way!

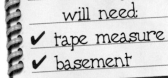

Things you will need:
- ✔ tape measure
- ✔ basement

Let's Get Started!

1. Measure the distance between the basement floor and the underside of the floor above. You can do this in the same way you measured the height of a ceiling. Or you can use a tape measure to measure the same distance.

2. Of course, the floor above the basement has thickness. This adds to to the depth of the basement. To find the thickness of the floor, look for a place where the end of the floor is exposed. Such an exposure can usually be found at the top of the stairs.

Suppose the distance between the basement floor and the bottom of the floor above is 2.30 meters, or 230 centimeters. If the thickness of the floor is

2.5 centimeters, then the depth of the basement is:

230 centimeters + 2.5 centimeters =

232.5 centimeters, or 92 inches

What fraction of the basement's depth is the thickness of the floor above?

Ideas for Your Science Fair

Are all basements the same depth? How can you find out? Do you find that newer homes have basements with higher ceilings?

How Deep Is a

Things you
will need:
- ✔ an ADULT
- ✔ pond or lake
- ✔ long string
- ✔ lead sinker
- ✔ life jacket
- ✔ dock or boat
- ✔ yarn
- ✔ tape measure

Ask an **adult** to help you with this activity.

Let's Get Started!

① Tie a long string to a lead sinker, such as the kind used by fishermen. **Put on a life jacket**.

② From a dock or boat, lower the lead sinker into the water.

③ When the sinker stops falling, mark the point where the water level meets the string. You can do this by tying a piece of yarn to the string. (If you are measuring from a dock, use a tape measure to measure the distance from the dock to the water. Then use your thumb and finger to grasp the string at the level of the dock. Tie the yarn to the string at a distance equal to the distance of the water below the dock.)

④ Pull the sinker out of the water.

⑤ On land, lay out the string and sinker. Stretch the string until it is straight. Then measure the distance from the bottom of the sinker to the mark on the string. What will this measurement tell you?

Pond or Lake?

How can you find out where the pond or lake is deepest? How deep is it?

Early Americans dug wells and lined them with stones. They lowered a bucket into the well and used it to raise water from the well. How could you measure the depth of the well? How could you measure the depth of the water in the well?

What Is the

As you know, Earth is a large sphere (ball). Most of what we see and know as Earth is on the surface of that sphere. Starting at Earth's surface, how far down could we go? A lot farther than your basement! There is a mine in South Africa that is 3.7 kilometers (2.3 miles) deep. The deepest borehole that geologists have made is 14.5 kilometers (9 miles) deep.

In theory, the deepest hole we could dig would be to the center of Earth. This drawing of Earth was made to scale. The artist drew it so that each centimeter represents 1,000 kilometers (620 miles).

Let's Get Started!

1. Use a ruler to find the distance to the center of Earth. In theory, what is the deepest hole we could dig?

2. The longest hole we could dig, in theory, would go through Earth to the other side. How long would that hole be?

Things you will need:
✓ ruler

Farthest "Down?"

Words to Know

air pressure—The force that air exerts over a certain area. This force occurs because of air's weight.

altimeter—A device used to measure altitude (height). There are two types. One type, which uses a barometer, is based on the fact that air pressure decreases with height above sea level. A second type uses radar and measures the time for a pulse of radio waves to travel to the ground and back.

aneroid barometer—A device used to measure air pressure.

borehole—A hole drilled in the earth.

clapboards—Long narrow boards used for siding the outside of a home.

estimate—To guess about or calculate roughly.

millibar—A unit of pressure. One millibar is approximately $\frac{1}{1,000}$ the pressure of air at sea level.

radar—A method of finding distance by measuring the time for a pulse of high-frequency radio waves to travel to and from an object or surface.

risers—The separation in height between steps in a flight of stairs.

skyscraper—A very tall building.

Answers

p. 15

169 meters – 10 meters = 159 meters;

159 meters x 100 centimeters/meter =

15,900 centimeters

15,900 centimeters ÷ 898 steps =

17.7 centimeters (or 7 inches)

p. 32

You assumed the covers were equal in thickness.

Further Reading

Books

Barner, Bob. *How to Weigh an Elephant*. New York: Bantam Books, 1995.

Bombaugh, Ruth. *Science Fair Success, Revised and Expanded*. Springfield, N.J.: Enslow Publishers, Inc., 1999.

Cook, Nancy, and Christine V. Johnson. *Measuring Dinosaurs*. Reading, Mass.: Addison-Wesley, 1995.

Gardner, Robert. *Science Project Ideas About the Moon*. Springfield, N.J.: Enslow Publishers, Inc., 1997.

————. *Science Project Ideas About Trees*. Springfield, N.J.: Enslow Publishers, Inc., 1997.

Markle, Sandra. *Measuring Up: Experiments, Puzzles, and Games Exploring Measurement*. New York: Atheneum, 1995.

Sharp, Richard M., and Seymour Metzner. *The Sneaky Square and 113 Other Math Activities for Kids*. Blue Ridge Summit, Pa.: TAB, 1990.

Smoothey, Marion. *Estimating*. New York: Marshall Cavendish, 1994.

Walpole, Brenda. *Distance*. Milwaukee, Wisc.: Gareth Stevens, 1995.

Internet Addresses

The Exploratorium. "The Science Explorer." <http://www.exploratorium.edu/science_explorer/>

Hunkins, Tim. "Height." <http://www.hunkinsexperiments.com/>

Scifair.org. "The Ultimate Science Fair Resource." © 2000. <http://www.scifair.org>

Index